DOMINION OVER
SICKNESS AND DISEASE

DOMINION OVER SICKNESS AND DISEASE

JONATHAN SHUTTLESWORTH

CONTENTS

Book design by eBook Prep
www.ebookprep.com
Cover design by Justin Stewart
www.justifii.com

February, 2020
ISBN: 978-1-64457-143-9

Rise UP Publications
644 Shrewsbury Commons Ave
Ste 249
Shrewsbury PA 17361
United States of America
www.riseUPpublications.com
Phone: 866-846-5123

A VERY IMPORTANT INTRODUCTION

In my time traveling this planet as a Minister of The Gospel of Jesus Christ, two things have stood out more than anything else.

> The heartbreaking stories of lovely men and women who have been victimized by The Devil. One horrific story after another; people created in the image of God rendered helpless by Satan's power.

> The supremacy of Christ's power to destroy all the devil's work, rendering his attacks powerless. Time and again, those with no hope, even given up to die, have their story gloriously rewritten by Jesus.

One of Satan's favorite ways to victimize mankind is through sickness and disease. With all the advancements of modern medicine, many are as helpless as they would have been 2,000 years ago! Their only hope is Jesus. Yet, just like 2,000 years ago, religious leaders have seeded doubt into their hearts, claiming God no longer does the miracles of The Bible. What foolishness!

God NEVER changes! Jesus Christ is the same, yesterday, today and forever! Furthermore, Christ's commission to those in ministry has never changed: wherever you go to preach—heal the sick.

This book is a potent exploration of God's nature and magnanimous healing power. Perhaps you have been victimized in your health? I've written this to you. This book does not merely contain information. It contains the revelation of The Risen Christ that has brought complete transformation and immediate help to the suffering for thousands of years.

I've broken this book into three sections. Christ's dominion over all four categories of sickness and disease; thirteen pillars of divine healing, and six reasons you can expect God to heal you immediately.

Even if you are reading this on a hospice bed, I believe God will raise you up. Anything damaged in your body can be healed and anything too damaged to be healed can be replaced.

Many great healing evangelists were given up to die. When they received their healing, they carried unshakable confidence in God's power to heal others. I believe you will join their ranks! Truly, what The Devil meant for bad, God will turn to good. Satan will rue the day he didn't kill you when he had the chance.

God created the whole world in six days; He won't need more than one hour to solve your troubles.

There's nothing The Devil has done to you that God can't do something about TODAY.

Love Always,

Jonathan

THE FOUR CATEGORIES OF SICKNESS AND DISEASE

I n our family, we call the eighth chapter of Matthew, the healing chapter of the New Testament. In the first seventeen verses, Jesus takes dominion over all sickness and all disease.

All sickness and all disease can be broken into four categories, and Jesus dominates all four—dominion He also gave His Church, which is His Body.

Large crowds followed Jesus as he came down the mountainside. Suddenly a man with leprosy approached him and knelt before him. Lord, the man said, I know if you want to, you can heal me and make me clean. Jesus reached out his hand and touched the man. "I am willing," he said. "Be clean!" Immediately he was cleansed of his leprosy.

— MATTHEW 8:1-3 (NLT)

Before Jesus healed the leper, He corrected him because Jesus has no favorites. The Bible says in Acts 10:34 that God is no respecter of persons. So, when Jesus answered this man's question, He answered everyone who would wonder, is it God's will to heal me?

"Lord," the man said, "I know if you want to, you can heal me and make me clean."

This is what trips up so many people. They know God can heal, but they're not sure if he'll do it for them. But when Jesus answered this man, He also answered you.

"I am willing," Jesus said.

And I want you to know that if you need healing or you desire healing, you never have to wonder how Jesus feels about it. He wants to.

"I am willing," He said, "be clean," and instantly the leprosy disappeared. Then Jesus said to him, "See that you don't tell anyone. But go, show yourself to the priest and offer the gift Moses commanded, as a testimony to them."

When Jesus returned to Capernaum a Roman officer came and pleaded with him, "Lord, my young servant lies in bed paralyzed and in terrible pain."

Jesus said, "I will come and heal him."

But the officer said, "I'm not worthy to have you come into my home. Just say the word from where you are and my servant will be healed. I know this because I am under the authority of my superior officers, and I have authority over my soldiers. I only need to say, 'Go,' and they go, or 'Come,' and they come. And if I say to my slaves, 'Do this,' they do it."

When Jesus heard this, he was amazed. Turning to those who were following him, he said, "I tell you the truth, I haven't seen faith like this in all Israel! And I tell you this, that many Gentiles will come from all over the world—from east and west—and sit down with Abraham, Isaac, and Jacob at the feast in the Kingdom of Heaven. But many Israelites—those for whom the Kingdom was prepared—will be thrown into outer darkness, where there will be weeping and gnashing of teeth."

Then Jesus said to the Roman officer, "Go back home. Because you believed, it has happened." And the young servant was healed that same hour.

When Jesus arrived at Peter's house, Peter's mother-in-law was sick in bed with a high fever. But when Jesus touched her hand, the fever left her. Then she got up and prepared a meal for him.

That evening many demon-possessed people were brought to Jesus. He cast out the evil spirits with a simple command, and he healed all the sick. This fulfilled the word of the Lord through the prophet Isaiah, who said, "He took (*not will take, not is taking, he took*) our sicknesses and removed (*not is removing, not will remove, he removed*) our diseases."

Jesus took our sicknesses and removed our diseases.

There are four categories in which all sickness and disease fall, and Jesus dominated all four.

FLESH AND PHYSICAL STRUCTURE

Leprosy decays the skin, decays joints, decays knees, decays discs and bone. Anything that attacks the structural makeup of the body, the flesh, and the skin, Jesus healed it.

NERVOUS SYSTEM

"My servant lies in bed paralyzed and in terrible pain"— diseases that attack the body's nervous systems, Parkinson's disease, multiple sclerosis, fibromyalgia. Jesus spoke the word and the disease left him.

BLOOD DISORDERS

Peter's mother-in-law was sick in bed with a high fever and Jesus touched her hand. Another translation says He spoke to the fever. Fevers reside in the blood. HIV, hepatitis A, B, and C, sickle cell anemia, any disease that's in the blood, Jesus spoke and it was healed.

DEMONIC SPIRITS

That evening they brought unto Jesus many who were sick and who were possessed by demons.

In about one out of every three people whom Jesus healed, a demon had to be dealt with. Thou spirit of infirmity (Luke 13:11), thou spirit that makes this boy deaf and mute (Mark 9:25). There's a category of demons that work to afflict bodies.

That's why there's still people today, even with all the advancements in medical science, who go to the doctor and hear "we don't have any clue why this is happening, we don't know how to treat it, we've never seen this happen before." It's because those demons Jesus dealt with back then never died. And they still look to afflict people today. But thankfully the same power Christ used to destroy their hold on the human body has been given to the believer today.

Any disease or sickness you're battling, or have battled, or you've come in contact with when ministering to the sick, will fall into one of those four categories. Jesus took care of all four, easily, and He gave His Church the same dominion.

THE THIRTEEN PILLARS OF DIVINE HEALING

E ach of these thirteen pillars from God's Word can stand alone, and you can put your faith in any one of them to receive divine healing.

But knowing and understanding all thirteen will make your faith unshakable because you're not basing divine healing on just one verse. It'll sound laughable for anyone to question divine healing after you see this from God's word.

1: SICKNESS IS FROM THE DEVIL

Sickness is not part of life or old age. That's the first thing you have to shake off because the world trains you, and in church they train you, that sickness and disease are part of life.

You hear, "Well, you know I'm turning fifty now, and the eyes are the first thing to go. When it turns Winter, I always get sick. When it's Spring, my allergies act up."

When you see sickness and disease as part of life, you'll always have it.

When you see sickness and disease as something that comes from the devil, a strength will rise up in your spirit to attack it and throw it out of your life, and out of other people's lives, too.

How do you know sickness and disease are from the devil? Here are three scriptures that clearly identify the author of sickness and disease.

"Then Satan went forth from the presence of God and smote Job with boils."

— JOB 2:7

Many people like to interpret the book of Job as the book where God stopped blessing people and started to curse people, instead.

Then there are people who will tell you God made Job sick. God was *not* the author of Job's sickness. In fact, in the last chapter of Job, God restored double to Job everything he lost.

Job 2:7 clearly states "Then Satan went forth from the presence of God and smote Job with boils."

Satan was the author of Job's sickness and disease.

> *"One Sabbath day as Jesus was teaching in a synagogue, he saw a woman who had been crippled by an evil spirit. She had been bent double for eighteen years and was unable to stand up straight. When Jesus saw her, he called her over and said, "Dear woman, you are healed of your sickness!" Then he touched her, and instantly she could stand straight. How she praised God!"*
>
> — LUKE 13: 10-13 (NLT)

Notice God didn't receive glory when she was sick, as some people teach. God received glory when she was healed.

"But the leader in charge of the synagogue was indignant that Jesus had healed her on the Sabbath day. "There are six days of the week for working," he said to the crowd. "Come on those days to be healed, not on the Sabbath."

But the Lord replied, "You hypocrites! Each of you works on the Sabbath day! Don't you untie your ox or your donkey from its stall on the Sabbath and lead it out for water? This dear woman, a daughter of Abraham, has been held in bondage by Satan for eighteen years." (Luke 13: 14-15, (NLT))

Jesus clearly identified Satan as the author of that woman's infirmity. An evil spirit had crippled her directly, and Satan indirectly. Satan was the author of her problem.

> *"And you know that God anointed Jesus of Nazareth with the Holy Spirit and with power. Then Jesus went around doing good and healing all who were oppressed by the devil, for God was with him."*
>
> — ACTS 10:38 (NLT)

Don't ever let anybody mislead you. God's *not* the author of 'bad.' God is the author of 'good.'

Jesus said, "The thief comes to steal, kill, and destroy but I have come that you might have life and have it more abundantly." (John 10:10)

Satan steals. Satan kills. Satan destroys. Jesus brings life.

Jesus went about doing good and healing *all*. How many does God want to heal? *All* oppressed by the devil. The devil is the oppressor.

As Nigerian pastor Iorista Jaafar says, "God is a good God and the devil is a bad devil."

Activate your faith for divine healing by settling that sicknesses is from the devil. Sickness is not an inevitable part of life and not an expected part of old age.

There's no record of the disciples being sick on their tour with Jesus. No record of Jesus having to cancel His trip to Capernaum because His allergies were flaring up.

Sickness is from the devil. It is not a part of life or a part of old age.

2: SICKNESS IS A CURSE, NOT A BLESSING

Christ has redeemed us from all the curse of the law.

— GALATIANS 3:13

Sickness is a curse, not a blessing.

In Deuteronomy 28:15-68 the curse of the law is outlined. If you read through that passage and underline everything God said is a curse, you'll find sickness and disease all through it. Blindness, tumors, scurvy, fever, blight, and mildew—which speaks of a virus and bacteria.

Then, in verse 61, it goes on to say, "and every sickness and plague there is, even those not mentioned in this book of the law..."

So, the Bible clearly states that *all* sickness and disease, even those not specifically mentioned in the curse of the law, is a curse and specifically part of the curse of the law.

But we have been redeemed.

Galatians 3:13 (KJV) says, "Christ hath redeemed us from the curse of the law, being made a curse for us: for it is written, Cursed is every one that hangeth on a tree."

So many people have only been taught part of what Christ did. They know Jesus died so our sins can be forgiven. Which is true. And if that's the only reason He died, that alone would be great.

But that's not the only reason Jesus died. The Bible says He died to redeem us from the curse of the law and sickness and disease, including every sickness and disease there is, even those not mentioned specifically in the Bible.

Matthew 8:17(NIV) says "He took up our infirmities and bore our diseases." Every sickness and disease that was meant to be laid on me, was laid on Christ. Every sickness and disease meant to be laid on you was laid on Christ. It's illegal for the devil to lay on you what Jesus has already taken in your place. You don't have to double pay for groceries. You don't have to double buy a car; it only has to be paid for once, no matter who paid for it.

Jesus paid the penalty for you to walk free from all sickness and all diseases. See it that way!

Don't say "Oh Lord, please heal me!" No. Two thousand years ago, Jesus TOOK all your sickness. He took all your disease. The devil can't lay it on you because it's already been laid on Christ Jesus.

Therefore, you are healed!

This is why, upon hearing the Biblical truth of divine healing, people would just get up out of their wheelchairs. They understood that Jesus took it, and they don't have to take it anymore.

So, if there's any sickness or disease in your body, receive your healing right now in Jesus' name. Christ already accomplished everything that needs to be done.

The price has been paid. Healing is yours.

3: WE HAVE THE BLESSING OF ABRAHAM

That the blessing of Abraham might come on the Gentiles through Jesus Christ; that we might receive the promise of the Spirit through faith.

— GALATIANS 3:14

You and I not only have the curse broken off our lives, we have also received the blessing of Abraham.

Galatians 3:14 says that He redeemed us in order that the blessing given to Abraham might come to the Gentiles through Christ Jesus.

How was Abraham blessed? How was Isaac blessed? How was Jacob blessed? All our covenant forefathers overshot their 120th birthday. They not only were free of sickness and disease; they were unusually healthy.

In his old age, Abraham led men out to battle. He became a father at a hundred years old, which means he was raising a 15-year-old boy at one-hundred-fifteen years of age. Most people in their twenties can't raise a five-year-old. Abraham was one-hundred-five raising a five-year-old. Before I had a child, I used to think about how amazing it was that Abraham became a father at a hundred. Now that I am a father, I think the greater miracle is raising a child in your hundreds— Abraham did that by the blessing from God.

When Moses was 120 years old, Deuteronomy 34:7 tells us

his eyes were not dim, and his strength was not abated. This is the inheritance of all who served the Lord.

Caleb, one of the 12 spies who scoped out the Promise Land, told Joshua, "I was forty years old when Moses, the servant of the Lord, sent me from Kadesh-Barnea to explore the land of Canaan. I returned and gave an honest report... So that day Moses solemnly promised me, 'The land of Canaan on which you were just walking will be your grant of land and that of your descendants forever, because you wholeheartedly followed the Lord my God.'

"Now, as you can see, the Lord has kept me alive and well as he promised for all these forty-five years since Moses made this promise—even while Israel wandered in the wilderness. Today I am eighty-five years old. I am as strong now as I was when Moses sent me on that journey, and I can still travel and fight as well as I could then. So give me the hill country that the Lord promised me." (Joshua 19 7, 9-12a (NLT))

At 85 years old, Caleb, by the blessing of God, was getting ready to take the greatest ground he had ever taken.

This blessing of Abraham—supernatural physical vitality and health even in old age—has been given to all believers.

4: GOD PROMISES HIS SERVANTS PROTECTION FROM SICKNESS AND DISEASE

"Then Moses led the people of Israel away from the Red Sea, and they moved out into the desert of Shur. They traveled in this desert for three days without

finding any water. When they came to the oasis of Marah, the water was too bitter to drink. So they called the place Marah (which means "bitter").

"Then the people complained and turned against Moses. "What are we going to drink?" they demanded. So Moses cried out to the Lord for help, and the Lord showed him a piece of wood. Moses threw it into the water, and this made the water good to drink.

"It was there at Marah that the Lord set before them the following decree as a standard to test their faithfulness to him. He said, "If you will listen carefully to the voice of the Lord your God and do what is right in his sight, obeying his commands and keeping all his decrees, then I will not make you suffer any of the diseases I sent on the Egyptians; for I am the Lord who heals you."

— EXODUS 15:22-26 (NLT)

The King James Version translates the last verse this way: "If thou wilt diligently hearken to the voice of the Lord thy God, and wilt do that which is right in his sight, and wilt give ear to his commandments, and keep all his statutes, I will put none of these diseases upon thee, which I have brought upon the Egyptians: for I am the Lord that healeth thee."

Exodus 23:25-26 further expounds upon the promise. "And ye shall serve the Lord your God, and he shall bless thy bread, and thy water; and I will take sickness away from the midst of thee. There shall nothing cast their young, nor be barren, in thy land: the number of thy days I will fulfill."

God not only promised healing and physical vitality. God promises protection from all sickness and disease for those who serve him diligently.

Did you hear that? God did *not* say "I'll heal you when you get sick." He said, "If you serve me, I will clear sickness and disease out of your midst. I'll bless your bread and water. Anything that would bring sickness and disease, I'll touch it and bless it and won't allow it to come in your direction."

So it's not "how many of you know God will heal you when you get sick?"

It's not "how many of you know sometimes God allows sickness because you can never know him as healer until you get sick." What stupidity!

God said, if you serve me, I will not allow any sickness or disease to come into your midst. I'll be a supernatural force field around you and will not allow any sickness or disease to come near you for I am the Lord your God who healeth thee.

Exodus 15 provides the illustration. The Israelites were wandering the desert and came upon water that was full of bacteria, or viruses, something that made the water so bitter when they drank it, even though they were thirsty, they spit it out. Then God showed Moses a piece of wood. DL. Moody purported the wood was a foreshadowing of the cross because you don't clear bitter water by throwing a stick into it. Moses took the wood by prophetic instruction, threw it in the water, and everything that made the water bitter to drink cleared out.

But God didn't just clear the water so the Israelites could drink. He said, now let this be an object lesson. If you serve me (and I hope you've made a decision to serve the Lord) the same way I cleared all that junk out of the water, I will clear out all virus, all bacteria, all sickness and disease out of your midst, for I am the Lord your God who heals you.

God promises protection from sickness and disease for the believer who diligently seeks him.

5: FAITH CARRIES THE CAPACITY TO OVERCOME SICKNESS AND DISEASE

"...the people followed, crowding around him [Jesus]. A woman in the crowd had suffered for twelve years with constant bleeding. She had suffered a great deal from many doctors, and over the years she had spent everything she had to pay them, but she had gotten no better. In fact, she had gotten worse. She had heard about Jesus, so she came up behind him through the crowd and touched his robe. For she thought to herself, "If I can just touch his robe, I will be healed." Immediately the bleeding stopped, and she could feel in her body that she had been healed of her terrible condition.

Jesus realized at once that healing power had gone out from him, so he turned around in the crowd and asked, "Who touched my robe?"

His disciples said to him, "Look at this crowd pressing around you. How can you ask, 'Who touched me?'"

But he kept on looking around to see who had done it. Then the frightened woman, trembling at the realization of what had happened to her, came and fell

*to her knees in front of him and told him what she had
done. And he said to her, "Daughter, your faith has
made you well...."*

— MARK 5:24-34A (NLT)

Faith in God draws on God's power and carries the capacity
to clear out all sickness and disease and make you well.

Romans 4:16, from the Amplified Bible says "Therefore,
inheriting the promise depends entirely on faith [that is, confi-
dent trust in the unseen God], in order that *it may be given* as
an act of grace [His unmerited favor and mercy], so that the
promise will be legally guaranteed to all the descendants of
Abraham—not only for those who keep the Law [Jewish
believers], but also for those [Gentile believers] who share
the faith of Abraham, who is the spiritual father of us all."

Then, starting in verse 18, we are given the object lesson of
that faith in action. "In hope against hope Abraham believed
that he would become a father of many nations, as he had
been promised by God: "So numberless shall your descendants be."

Without becoming weak in faith, he [Abraham] considered
his own body, now as good as dead for producing children
since he was about a hundred years old, and he considered the
deadness of Sarah's womb.

But he did not doubt *or* waver in unbelief concerning the
promise of God, but he grew strong *and* empowered by faith,
giving glory to God, being fully convinced that God had the
power to do what He had promised. Therefore, his faith was
credited to him as righteousness (right standing with God)."

Now, if a hundred-year-old man wanted to father a baby, today, the medical community would say, "tough luck. You should've come to the clinic 40 years ago. Then *maybe* we could've helped you."

But Abraham, even though he and his wife Sarah were well-beyond the age of having a baby, believed those things which were spoken unto him by God, and God counted it as right-eousness. As a result, Abraham's body grew strong and was empowered by faith.

Many denominations teach that the Power (including the power to heal) which filled the believers in the Book of Acts died with the last apostle.

Even if that were true, and it's not true, but even if it were true that the Holy Spirit no longer heals through believers, Jesus did *not* say to the woman healed from the issue of blood, "daughter, be encouraged, the Holy Ghost has made you well." Jesus said, "daughter, be encouraged, your *faith* has made you well."

Say this out loud: **My faith has made me well.**

Even if those who say "we don't believe the Holy Spirit does that anymore. We believe that work of the Holy Spirit has died out" are right—and they're *not* right—has faith died out? If it has, we're all going to hell because the Bible says it is by grace you are saved through *faith*. (Ephesians 2:8) Nobody in their right mind who has a first-grade Sunday school educa-tion teaches that faith has died out.

If the devil can get you to consider your own body, you'll never receive healing; never go by how you feel. You have to hold God's Word. We walk by faith and not by sight. (2 Corinthians 5:7)

Faith, by itself, carries the capacity to draw on God's healing power for your body.

6: THE ANOINTING INCAPACITATES SICKNESS, DISEASE, AND DEMON SPIRITS

"After the Philistines captured the Ark of God, they took it from the battleground at Ebenezer to the town of Ashdod. They carried the Ark of God into the temple of Dagon and placed it beside an idol of Dagon. But when the citizens of Ashdod went to see it the next morning, Dagon had fallen with his face to the ground in front of the Ark of the Lord! So, they took Dagon and put him in his place again. But the next morning the same thing happened—Dagon had fallen face down before the Ark of the Lord again. This time his head and hands had broken off and were lying in the doorway. Only the trunk of his body was left intact."

— 1 SAMUEL 5:1-4 (NLT)

What was in that Ark that caused that idol to fall down? The Ark of the Covenant (or the Ark of God) carried the manifest presence of God. It carried the anointing.

But it was never God's desire to dwell in vessels made by human hands.

The Apostle Paul wrote in 1 Corinthians 6:19, "...know ye not that your body is the temple of the Holy Ghost which is in you, which ye have of God..."

In Pillar #5, I pointed out that even if the Holy Spirit is no longer doing what He did in the Book of Acts, faith by itself carries the capacity to get you well. But thank God the Holy Spirit has *not* left the earth!

The same Holy Spirit that worked in the apostles and the Church in the Book of Acts is available to everyone who believes and abides in him.

Just like the Holy Spirit effortlessly leveled the Philistines' idol of Dagon, the strongest power the devil has at his disposal cannot stand in His presence.

If you have received the Holy Spirit, you have received an anointing from the Holy One. (1 John) You are anointed.

Say this out loud: **I am anointed.**

What was in the Ark of the Covenant dwells in you, the same anointing so potent in the Apostle Paul that the clothing which touched his skin was stronger than any sickness or disease or any demon spirit. (Acts 19:11)

My friend, an anointed believer doesn't have to pull somebody demon possessed into a back room and pray for six hours. The residue of the anointing in the cotton or wool or whatever material you have on is stronger than the strongest demon. Stronger than death, stronger than disease, stronger than demon spirits!

The Psalmist said in Psalm 92, "I will be anointed with fresh oil."

As you stay in the presence of God, the power of the Holy Ghost in you, and flowing through you, effortlessly destroys all sickness and all disease.

Now, put Pillars 5 and 6 together: I have faith in God's Word and I am anointed.

That's your 'C4 and a detonator' against all sickness and all disease.

7: JESUS' BLOOD HAS POWER

And if one prevail against him, two shall withstand him; and a threefold cord is not quickly broken.

— ECCLESIASTES 4:12

The Bible says in Ecclesiastes 4:12 that a threefold cord is not easily broken.

So, if you take the inherent power faith carries, entwine it with the anointing of the Holy Spirit, and the blood of Jesus sprinkled over us (Hebrews 12:24) you have a threefold cord that cannot be broken.

Isaiah 53:1-5 (NLT) says, "Who has believed our message? To whom has the Lord revealed his powerful arm?

My servant grew up in the Lord's presence like a tender green shoot, like a root in dry ground. There was nothing beautiful or majestic about his appearance, nothing to attract us to him. He was despised and rejected—a man of sorrows, acquainted with deepest grief.

We turned our backs on him and looked the other way. He was despised, and we did not care. Yet it was our weaknesses he carried; it was our sorrows that weighed him down. And we thought his troubles were a punishment from God, a punishment for his own sins!

But he was pierced for our rebellion, crushed for our sins. He was beaten so we could be whole. He was whipped so we could be healed."

The Amplified Bible translates the last phrase of Isaiah 53:5 this way: "…and by his stripes we are healed."

Now, look at 1 Peter 2:24. "Who his own self bare our sins in his own body on the tree, that we, being dead to sins, should live unto righteousness: by whose stripes ye were healed."

In the Old Testament, Isaiah is foreshadowing what Christ was going to do.

In the New Testament, Peter is looking back on what Jesus had done.

Note what Peter said: "By whose stripes you *were* healed". He didn't say you *will* be healed…

Some people say, "I really need a healing. I'm believing God's going to heal me someday…"

No, you need to understand Jesus *already did* what needed to be done. Just like there's nothing left for Him to do to save you, He's *already taken* the stripes upon his back for you to be healed.

Physical healing is part of the redemptive work of Christ. By his stripes, you are healed! (Isaiah 53:5, Matthew 8:17)

Now, there are denominations and some churches that say, "well, no, those verses mean we were spiritually sick and by His stripes we were healed of our spiritual sickness, our sin."

But that's wrong!

Jesus was not whipped after the cross. He was whipped before the cross. If His stripes purchased our freedom from sin, then there was no reason for Him to go to the cross.

He was beaten that we might have peace. Our chastisement was laid upon him and by his stripes we were healed of our physical sicknesses and diseases.

Matthew said, in Matthew 8:16-17, "he [Jesus] did this [healed all the sick brought to him], that it might be fulfilled what was spoken by the prophet Isaiah, that by his stripes we are healed."

If I *were* healed, then I *is* healed. If I *was* healed, I *am* healed. Why? Because He already did it.

That is the healing power of the Blood of Jesus.

But it doesn't stop there.

In the twelfth chapter of Exodus the Israelites are slaves to the Egyptians who have endured nine plagues but still refuse to let God's people go. Now the death angel, the strongest angel at the devil's disposal, is ordered to go door to door and kill the firstborn of every home. You didn't avoid the death angel that night because you were Hebrew. You avoided the death angel because you acted upon the prophetic instruction given to Moses to take a lamb without blemish, without spot or wrinkle, kill it without breaking any of its bones, drain its blood into a basin, then with hyssop branches apply the blood to the doorpost of your house. "And when I see the blood, I will pass over you."

This is the origin of the Jewish Passover.

Any theology book you read, Baptist, Pentecostal, Presbyterian, Catholic, will tell you the same thing: the blood of that lamb without spot or wrinkle is a type of (or foreshadowing of) Christ and His blood that warded off not a type of the death angel but the actual death angel.

So, I have a question for you. If the blood that *represented* the blood of Jesus had power to ward off death, how much more power is there in the actual blood of Jesus that the Bible says in Hebrews was sprinkled over us?

It serves as a glowing red neon sign to the devil. You can't touch her. You can't touch him. He is redeemed. She is redeemed. You are redeemed from all sickness, all disease, and all the devil's power.

That is the power of the Blood of Jesus!

8: UNDERSTAND THE POWER OF GOD'S WORD

"My child, pay attention to what I say. Listen carefully to my words. Don't lose sight of them. Let them penetrate deep into your heart, for they bring life to those who find them, and healing to their whole body."

— PROVERBS 4:20-22 (NLT)

God's word is not a natural book. God's Word is a healing balm, the supernatural breath of God. The Word is God-breathed.

When you read the Bible it's not like reading a regular book.

Reading the God's Word infuses the life of God into your body and brings life, radiant healing, and wholeness to your whole being.

There's a preacher I know who had a lump, a growth, develop in his neck, and the doctors planned to operate. Then one day, the preacher got mad because he understood from the Bible what I understand, that he shouldn't have to put up with this.

So, every day, he would read Isaiah 53, then lay his open Bible on the growth and say "thank you Father that your word carries healing power."

Two weeks later, he went for the pre-surgery scan so the doctors would know where to cut. But when they examined the scan, they discovered the growth was reduced by 80%, and the other 20% was dying.

God's Word brings radiant health and healing to the body of the one who attends unto it.

9: UNDERSTAND THE POWER IN JESUS' NAME

"...thou shalt call his name Jesus: for he shall save his people from their sins."

— MATTHEW 1:21B

Jesus was first given his name by the angel who appeared to Mary.

Jesus also earned his name through conquest.

Philippians 2:7-11 (NLT) says, "Instead, he [Jesus] gave up his divine privileges, he took the humble position of a slave and was born as a human being.

When he appeared in human form, he humbled himself in obedience to God and died a criminal's death on a cross.

Therefore, God elevated him to the place of highest honor and gave him the name above all other names, at the name of Jesus every knee should bow, in heaven and on earth and under the earth, and every tongue declare that Jesus Christ is Lord, the glory of God the Father."

Because Jesus left the Heights of Heaven and died a criminal's death on the cross, God raised him to new Heights in Heaven and gave Him a name above every name, such that at the very mention of Jesus' name, everything that's over the earth, on the earth, and under the earth has to bow at the mention of that name.

This was Jesus's reward for being obedient to death on the cross. His name carries power to subdue all other power, no matter where it resides.

Yeah, but don't those verses just mean people will bow on judgment day? Saying that all sickness and disease must bow at the mention of the name Jesus is taking it a bit too far, right?

Peter didn't think so.

In the third chapter of Acts, after Peter healed the crippled man, Peter took the opportunity to address the onlookers. He said "People of Israel, what is so surprising about this? And why stare at us as though we had made this man walk by our own power or godliness? For it is the God of Abraham, Isaac, and Jacob—the God of all our ancestors—who has brought glory to his servant Jesus by doing this. This is the same Jesus whom you handed over and rejected before Pilate, despite Pilate's decision to release him. You rejected this holy, righteous one and instead demanded the release of a murderer. You killed the author of life, but God raised him from the dead. And we are witnesses of this fact!

"Through faith in Jesus' name, this man was healed—and you know how crippled he was before. Faith in Jesus' name has healed him before your very eyes."

Jesus' name is full of wonders. Jesus' name has power. That's why, on secular television, producers and the like don't care if you say God. God is generic. God means a million things to a million people. But when you say Jesus' name they will not allow that name spoken on secular TV. It carries power!

When you speak Jesus' name, when people hear it, it's like a balloon pops over their heads, revealing undeniable signs and wonders "before their very eyes."

Understand the power that's in Jesus' name!

10: GOD'S COVENANT INCLUDES SUPERNATURAL STRENGTH IN OLD AGE

But you have made me as strong as a wild ox. You have anointed me with the finest oil.

— PSALM 92:10 (NLT)

38

Strength and the anointing go hand in hand in the Bible just like you see sin, sickness, disease, death, and demons go together.

Verses 12-14: "But the godly will flourish like palm trees and grow strong like the cedars of Lebanon. For they are transplanted to the Lord's own house. They flourish in the courts of our God. Even in old age they will still produce fruit; they will remain vital and green."

God's covenant includes supernatural strength in old age. "Even in old age, they will remain vital and green and shall produce much fruit."

But, the world prepares you to be sick in old age. 'Are you a man over the age of fifty? Are you a woman over the age of sixty?' Advertisements and TV commercials teach you to expect sickness and disease. Even from pulpits, people joke, 'well, you know, when I was young, I used to really think I could do anything. Now you start turning fifty-five or sixty... man that floor gets farther down every year.'

If you identify as a human being in this world, you'll have what human beings in this world have.

But, if you identify yourself using the way the Bible tells you to identify yourself, as a son of God, a daughter of God, with access to what He's given you, the Bible says "he has given us great and precious promises...that enable you to share his divine nature and escape the world's corruption caused by human desires." (2 Peter 1:4 (NLT)

God has given us power through his great and precious promises to rise above what the world tells us to expect of old age. "Even in old age, they will produce fruit."

God's plan is not for you to sit in the corner of a room with somebody feeding you vanilla pudding, your mind foggy. That's not scriptural. Abraham was unusually strong in old age. Elijah outran King Ahab's chariot as an old man because the hand of the Lord was upon him. (I Kings 18:46)

God's covenant with you does not just include healing.

God's covenant with you doesn't just include strength.

God's covenant with you includes *supernatural* strength. Even in old age as my days are, so shall my strength be.

"And Moses, though he was one-hundred-twenty years old, his eyes were not dim and his strength was unabated." (Deuteronomy 34:7) This is the inheritance of all who served the Lord.

11: UNDERSTAND THE MYSTERY OF A HEALTHY NATION

He brought them forth also with silver and gold: and there was not one feeble person among their tribes.

— PSALM 105:37

Over 3 million men, women, and children, old men, old women, and there was not one feeble or one sick among their tribes. Their clothing didn't wear out. Their feet never blistered or became swollen. God even kept their clothes laundered and their bodies from having natural problems.

But this was the Old Covenant.

Hebrews 8:6 says, "...for he [Jesus] is the one who mediates for us a far better covenant with God, based on better promises.

You have an even better covenant based on better promises than what they had in the Old Testament.

Say this out loud. **I have a better covenant based on better promises.**

So how much more can I expect to receive today from the hand of God?

12: UNDERSTAND THE HEALTHY TREE THAT IS JESUS

"...you were cut off from what is by nature a wild olive tree, and against nature were grafted into a cultivated olive tree..."

— ROMANS 11:24

You were a diseased branch in sin. But God has grafted you, into the healthy tree that is Jesus. When a diseased branch is grafted into a healthy tree, the disease does not overwhelm the tree. Instead, the health of the tree flows into the branch and overwhelms the disease.

The health of Jesus is flowing into you.

See yourself that way. See yourself as a branch that's now

connected to Christ. What is in Him is flowing into you driving out sickness and disease in Jesus' name.

Let me say that again. What flows through Him, flows into you. As He is, so you are in this world.

13: UNDERSTAND THE MYSTERY OF THE SERPENT IN THE WILDERNESS

Then the people of Israel set out from Mount Hor, taking the road to the Red Sea to go around the land of Edom. But the people grew impatient with the long journey, and they began to speak against God and Moses. "Why have you brought us out of Egypt to die here in the wilderness?" they complained. "There is nothing to eat here and nothing to drink. And we hate this horrible manna!"

So, the Lord sent poisonous snakes among the people, and many were bitten and died. Then the people came to Moses and cried out, "We have sinned by speaking against the Lord and against you. Pray that the Lord will take away the snakes." So Moses prayed for the people.

— NUMBERS 21:4-6 (NLT)

…and God just answered their prayer, right? No, this was God's answer.

Verses 8-9: "Then the Lord told him [Moses], "Make a

replica of a poisonous snake and attach it to a pole. All who are bitten will live if they simply look at it!" So Moses made a snake out of bronze and attached it to a pole. Then anyone who was bitten by a snake could look at the bronze snake and be healed!"

So, what pushed this supernaturally healthy tribe of people into sickness, disease, and death? Complaining and turning against God. "We have sinned by speaking against the Lord and against you." Their sin opened the door for this attack.

Here's what Jesus had to say about the bonze snake. John 3:14-15: "And as Moses lifted up the bronze snake on a pole in the wilderness, so the Son of Man must be lifted up, so that everyone who believes in him will have eternal life."

Jesus, like the bronze snake on the pole, represents healing and deliverance.

Did God tell the Israelites, "I forgive you of sinning, but you're still going to die of the snake bite"?

No. The Israelites who looked up at the bronze snake received healing from the sickness and disease brought by the snake which entered through the door of sin. Those who followed the prophetic instruction received forgiveness of spiritual sin (complaining and turning against God) and healing from what was attacking the body.

"So I, the son of man must be lifted up."

Simply look and live. Believe that Jesus became sickness and disease on the cross for you and you'll live. It's that easy.

"For God made Christ, who never sinned, to be the offering for our sin, so that we could be made right with God through Christ." (2 Corinthians 5:21 (NLT))

In Koine Greek, the original language in which the Book of Corinthians was written, the verse actually says "God made Christ who never sinned to become sin itself."

The sin that was on me, was put on Christ.

That's why God had to turn his face from His Son hanging on the cross at Calvary.

Jesus took my sin, Jesus took my sickness, as if it were His own.

Say this out loud: **Sin, sickness, and poverty** *passed from me* **to Calvary. Righteousness, healing, and prosperity** *passed from Calvary* **to me.**

Jesus took what was meant to be yours and mine so we can receive what belongs to Him: power and dominion over sickness, disease, and the devil.

SIX BIBLICAL REASONS WHY YOU CAN BE HEALED IMMEDIATELY

What keeps many people from receiving healing is they think 'in God's time', 'when He's ready'.

Jesus is always ready. Jesus is always willing. Jesus already paid the price for your healing.

Here are six Biblical reasons why you can expect to be healed immediately, today.

1: UNDERSTAND IMMEDIATELY

The word immediately is used fifty-five times in the Bible, all of which are in the New Testament. Most surround the miracle healing and deliverance ministry of Jesus.

Never was anyone in the Bible told to come back tomorrow or 'I'm not healing you today.' Immediately his eyes came open. Immediately the boy heard and spoke.

Jesus Christ has not changed. He is the same yesterday, today and forever. Understand immediately.

2: JESUS FEELS WHAT YOU FEEL

Matthew 8:16-17 (KJV) says, "When the even was come, they brought unto him [Jesus] many that were possessed with devils: and he cast out the spirits with his word, and healed all that were sick: that it might be fulfilled which was spoken by Esaias the prophet, saying, Himself took our infirmities, and bare our sicknesses."

Hebrews 4:15 (KJV) continues by showing the resurrected Jesus, seated next to the Father, "Seeing then that we have a great high priest, that is passed into the heavens, Jesus the Son of God, let us hold fast our profession. For we have not an high priest which cannot be touched with the feeling of our infirmities; but was in all points tempted like as we are, yet without sin.

Jesus put on a flesh body, lived in that human body. He feels what you feel. And He took on whatever you're battling. He took it to the cross with Him. He understands.

3: HE HAS COMPASSION

Isaiah 49:14: "Yet Jerusalem says, "The Lord has deserted us; the Lord has forgotten us."

Have you ever felt that way? Any time the devil tries to attack with sickness and disease, self-doubt often follows. It's Satan's two-pronged attack. He not only wants you to be sick, he wants you to think you did something to tick God off, or he's forgotten about you, or he's mad at you.

Here's God's response in verses 14-15: "Never! Can a mother forget her nursing child? Can she feel no love for the child she has borne? But even if that were possible, I would not forget you! See, I have written your name on the palms of my hands."

Jesus doesn't just feel what you feel. He has compassion about what you're going through. Understand that Jesus loves you.

Look at Jesus's response to two blind men sitting along the road in Matthew 20:29-33. "As Jesus and the disciples left the town of Jericho, a large crowd followed behind. Two blind men were sitting beside the road. When they heard that Jesus was coming that way, they began shouting, "Lord, Son of David, have mercy on us!"

"Be quiet!" the crowd yelled at them.

But they only shouted louder, "Lord, Son of David, have mercy on us!"

When Jesus heard them, he stopped and called, "What do you want me to do for you?"

"Lord," they said, "we want to see!" Jesus felt sorry for them and touched their eyes. Instantly they could see! Then they followed him.

Jesus had compassion on them. But it wasn't an empty compassion. His compassion moved Him to action.

You don't have some unfeeling idol, like the Dagon the Philistine god, that you serve. You have a compassionate Redeemer.

Understand His compassion. Study it. Discover it. Be consumed by it.

4: HEALING IS THE CHILDREN'S BREAD

It is God's responsibility to heal you and God is not delinquent in his responsibility.

1 Timothy 5:8 says, "if any provide not for his own, and specially for those of his own house, he hath denied the faith, and is worse than an infidel."

But God is three times Holy. "Holy, holy, holy is the Lord God, the Almighty—the one who always was, who is, and who is still to come." (Revelation 4:8)

God is not an infidel. He provides for His family, for His children.

His children's bread is healing, their daily provision.

Say this out loud: **Daily provision is my bread.**

"Give us this day our daily bread…" You don't have to wonder "will God heal me today?" There's daily bread already made available to you.

This is one of the things that got me healed years ago when I was battling something in my body. I was wondering when the Lord was going to heal me. Then I got this revelation that there's a daily provision of healing. Healing is the children's bread.

Take a look at the Gentile woman in Matthew 15 who approached Jesus about her tormented daughter. Now, during Jesus's earthly ministry, He was called to minister to the Jewish people. "A Gentile woman who lived there [Galilee] came to him [Jesus], pleading, "Have mercy on me, O Lord, Son of David! For my daughter is possessed by a demon that torments her severely."

48

But Jesus gave her no reply, not even a word. Then his disciples urged him to send her away. "Tell her to go away," they said. "She is bothering us with all her begging."

Then Jesus said to the woman, "I was sent only to help God's lost sheep—the people of Israel."

But she came and worshiped him, pleading again, "Lord, help me!"

Jesus responded, "It isn't right to take food from the children and throw it to the dogs."

She replied, "That's true, Lord, but even dogs are allowed to eat the scraps that fall beneath their masters' table."

"Dear woman," Jesus said to her, "your faith is great. Your request is granted." And her daughter was instantly healed."

Even the crumbs that fall from the children's table have the ability to expel all sickness and disease.

But now we are grafted into the Family of God, and we get more than just crumbs; we get to eat at the baker's table, we get the bread itself.

5: SICKNESS IS OPPRESSION FROM THE DEVIL

I John 3:8 (NLT) says, "But the Son of God came to destroy the works of the devil."

Sickness is from the devil. For this reason was the son of God made manifest that he might destroy the devil's work.

Was He able to accomplish it?

Isaiah 54:13-14 (KJV): "And all thy children shall be taught of the Lord; and great shall be the peace of thy children. In righteousness shalt thou be established: thou shalt be far from oppression; for thou shalt not fear: and from terror; for it shall not come near thee."

When Jesus said "it is finished," our battle against sickness and disease was finished. He accomplished the work.

Sicknesses and oppression are from the devil. Jesus came to destroy the devil's work and when he said it is finished, he completed it.

Isaiah 54 says "oppression, sicknesses"—according to Acts 10:38 sickness is oppression—"shall be far from you."

Sickness is not a continual battle.

6: GOD WANTS US TO ACT AND THINK LIKE HIM

Proverbs 3:27-28 (NLT): "Do not keep good from those who should have it, when it is in your power to do it. Do not say to your neighbor, "Go, and return tomorrow, and I will give it," when you have it with you. Do not plan for your neighbor to be hurt, while he trusts you enough to live beside you."

The sixth reason why you can expect God to heal you today: when God teaches us, or gives us instruction, He's directing us to act like Him and think like Him.

If it's in your power to help someone, don't tell them to come back tomorrow. Help them now.

Is it in God's power to help you today? Is God a hypocrite? No, He is not.

Then he won't tell you to come back tomorrow. He'll help you, and by "help" I mean He'll heal you today.

READER NOTES:

ABOUT JONATHAN SHUTTLESWORTH

Jonathan Shuttlesworth is an evangelist and founder of Revival Today, a ministry dedicated to reaching lost and hurting people with The Gospel of Jesus Christ.

In fulfilling his calling, Evangelist Shuttlesworth has conducted meetings and open-air crusades throughout North America, India, the Caribbean, and Central and South Africa. Each day thousands of lives are impacted globally through Revival Today Broadcasting located in Pittsburgh, Pennsylvania.

While methods may change, Revival Today's heartbeat remains for the lost, providing biblical teaching on faith, healing, prosperity, freedom from sin and living a victorious life.

If you need help or would like to partner with Revival Today to see this generation transformed through The Gospel, click the links below.

RevivalToday.com

facebook.com/revivaltoday

twitter.com/jdshuttlesworth

instagram.com/jdshuttlesworth

youtube.com/RevivalToday07

amazon.com/author/jonathanshuttlesworth

CPSIA information can be obtained
at www.ICGtesting.com
Printed in the USA
BVHW031136240922
647682BV00006B/29

9 781644 571439